All About Food Chains

by Kim Borland

Scott Foresman
is an imprint of

PEARSON

Glenview, Illinois • Boston, Massachusetts • Chandler, Arizona
Upper Saddle River, New Jersey

Every effort has been made to secure permission and provide appropriate credit for photographic material. The publisher deeply regrets any omission and pledges to correct errors called to its attention in subsequent editions.

Unless otherwise acknowledged, all photographs are the property of Pearson.

Photo locations denoted as follows: Top (T), Center (C), Bottom (B), Left (L), Right (R), Background (Bkgd)

Opener: (T) Brand X Pictures, (C) Getty Images; 1 (TR) Brand X Pictures, (CL) Getty Images; 3 (TL, TC, CR, BR) Getty Images, (BL) Digital Vision; 4 (L, R) Digital Vision; 5 Digital Vision; 6 (TL) Getty Images, (BR) Digital Vision; 7 Getty Images; 8 (CR, TL) Getty Images, (BC) Digital Vision; 9 Digital Vision; 11 Getty Images

ISBN 13: 978-0-328-50737-5
ISBN 10:   0-328-50737-7

Copyright © by Pearson Education, Inc., or its affiliates. All rights reserved.
Printed in the United States of America. This publication is protected by copyright, and permission should be obtained from the publisher prior to any prohibited reproduction, storage in a retrieval system, or transmission in any form or by any means, electronic, mechanical, photocopying, recording, or likewise. For information regarding permissions, write to Pearson Curriculum Rights & Permissions, One Lake Street, Upper Saddle River, New Jersey 07458.

Pearson® is a trademark, in the U.S. and/or in other countries, of Pearson plc or its affiliates.

Scott Foresman® is a trademark, in the U.S. and/or in other countries, of Pearson Education, Inc., or its affiliates.

3 4 5 6 V0N4 14 13 12 11 10

Living things are everywhere! Plants are living things. Animals are living things. You are a living thing too.

Living things require food. Food gives living things the energy they need to live and grow.

How many living things can you name? Which of these live on land? Which ones live in water?

Many living things eat other living things. This makes a food chain. Each living thing is a link in the food chain.

Food chains are found in every environment. They are all alike in one important way. Food chains begin with the sun and plants.

Sun

Bamboo

Did you know that most plants make their own food? It's true! They use the energy of the sun to make their food. When an animal eats the plant's leaves, energy is passed on. The sun's energy goes to the plant and then to the animal.

Panda

Let's take a close look at a forest. In a forest there are many food chains. The plants and animals can be part of more than one food chain. The plants and animals need each other to live.

Grass

Grasshopper

Some grasshoppers eat grass. A snake eats grasshoppers. The grass, the grasshopper, and the snake are linked. They form a food chain. Each plant and animal is a link in that chain.

Snake

A change in one part of the food chain causes a change in the other parts. What if there were no more grasshoppers?

The grasshoppers would not eat the grass. The grass might thrive, but the snakes would not have food. They could die if there was not enough to eat.

Food is a requirement of most living things. All living things are linked to other living things in food chains. As living things eat and are eaten, food chains go on. Food chains can change as environments change.

Now Try This

Living Things Poster

You know that living things are all around. Now it's your turn to share what you know about these living things!

Here's How to Do It!

1. Find a large sheet of white construction paper. Get some crayons too.
2. Write *Living Things* across the top of your paper.
3. Draw pictures of plants and animals that you know about. (Hint: They can be plants and animals that live on land or in water!)
4. Write the name of each plant or animal under its picture.
5. Share your drawings with your class.